Finding K :
The Great
Alphabet Hunt

Paula Curtis Taylorson

illustrated by Anastasia Kotelnikova

Finding K : The Great Alphabet Hunt

This is a work of fiction.

Printed in the United States of America

A 2 Z Press LLC

PO Box 582

Deleon Springs, FL 32130

bestlittleonlinebookstore.com

sizemore3630@aol.com

440-241-3126

ISBN: 978-1-954191-12-9

Dedication

*Thank you to those
who read to me and
those who listened
to me read.*

This book belongs to:

_____

Sir **Kanga Kendrick** is searching for **K** words.
He's well-**known** for the **knowledge** he **keeps**.

He's helped by his **kin**, **Kaiden** and **Kobe**,
Who are dressed as **knights**, they
stand guard while he sleeps.

In the **Kensington** Hotel in London,
the **kitchen's knee-deep** in fine food.

A cauldron of **kumquats** and **key** limes are mixed with some **kiwis** and stewed.

They've spotted a **kindly** old lady -
An expert in **Kendo** and **Kung** fu !

She's boiling a **kettle** for tea time,

And invited some **krill** that she **knew**.

In the distance is **Kilimanjaro,**

KILIMANJARO

It's a mountain that's fit for a **king**.

And right at the top is a **kiosk**,
where they sell **knickers**
and **ketchup** and string.

Kandinsky, the old Russian artist, paints a **khaki** green, polka dot **kitten.**

And a cute **kinkajou** who's called **Kenneth** asked,
'Do you **know** the way back to Great Britain?'

A **Komodo** dragon is playing a **keyboard,**

While a **Koala** bear plays the **kazoo**,

And a **killer** whale sings **karaoke**

To a **kangaroo** making Swiss cheese fondue.

They met John **Keats**, the a romantic poet,

And a nightingale sang as
Kathy kanga **knitted** a sweater,

that was a **kaleidoscope** of beautiful colours,

But the **kakapo** said he could have done better !

Kobi and Kim found a doorway,

and a sign saying **knickerbocker glory** this way !

Then, they got into a
go-**kart** and sped off,

Leaving the **kippers** to prepare a buffet.

'**Knock knock**, who's there?' 'It's **a knot**,' said Miss **Koo** the **kindergarten** teacher,

The **kite** won't be able to fly now,

So she climbed on the **kennel** to reach her !

A lady who is wearing a **kimono**,
Sits, watching the **koi**
swimming in **kelp**,

While a man with red **knuckles** and **knobbly knees**, shouts '**Kōkua!**' which is Hawaiian for 'Help !'

Sir **Kendrick's** the one with a **knapsack,**

And inside is the dictionary **key**,

It unlocks the **Ks** in
this alphabet hunt.
There's loads more if
you look carefully!

The End

My Very Own 'K' Words:

Glossary

Page 1. Kanga : a shortened name for kangaroo
Kendrik : male name in this book
Known : be aware, understand something
Knowledge : information possessed or have, aware of facts, truths, educated
Keeps : hold or retain as your own - a possession

Page 2. Kin : family member
Kaiden : a boy or man's name
Kobe : a boy or man's name
Knights : mounted soldier from the Middle ages

Page 3.. Kensington Hotel : a fancy hotel in London, England
Kitchen : room, location where food is prepared
Knee-deep : up to one's knee joint

Page 4. Kumquats : small citrus fruit
Key lime : a green citrus fruit
Kiwis : a fruit, food

Page 5. Kindly : good and generous nature, gentle, thoughtful, helpful, considerate
Kendo : Japanese form of fencing using bamboo staves
Kung fu : Chinese martial art

Page 6. Kettle : large metal pot for boiling liquids/water or cooking foods

Page 7. Krill : shrimp-like creatures, crustaceans
Knew : to be aware of, have information about

Page 8. **Kilimanjaro** : a volcanic mountain in North Tanzania - the highest peak in Africa, 19,321 feet

Page 9. **King** : a male ruler of a country or people

Page 10. **Kiosk** : a small structure with 1 or more open sides - for a newstand, refreshment stand, bandstand
Knickers : British - loose fitting short pants that gather at the knee
Ketchup : a condiment made of tomatoes, onions, vinegar, sugar, and spices

Page 11. **Kandinsky** : a famous Russian artist
Khaki : dull yellowish / green or brown color
Kitten :small or young cat

Page 12. **Kinkajou** : a small animal from Central or South America in the rain forest that resembles a raccoon or ferret
Kenneth : a boy or man's name
Know : to be aware of something, have information

Page 13. **Komodo dragon** : a large lizard
Keyboard : a row or set of keys in a piano or organ, a musical instrument

Page 14. **Koala** : a cute tree-living marsupial that resembles a teddy bear
Kazoo : a small musical instrument

Page 15. **Killer whale** : a large mammal that lives in the ocean
Karaoke : act of singing along to a music video or the words to a song with music only and you sing

Page 16. **Kangaroo** : a large marsupial that has long feet and a long tail and hops from Australia and New Guinea

Page 17. **Keats** : a famous poet from England

Page 18. **Kathy** : a girl or woman's name
Knitted : here - to make a garment, something with yarn and needles that you interlock the yarn in to hold the stiches together like a sweater

Page 19. **Kaleidoscope** : an optical instrument with bits of colored glass held loosely in a tube that rotates and are colorful and change shape and color

Page 20. **Kakapo** : a large flightless, nocturnal bird that is found in New Zealand and is endangered

Page 21. **Kobi** : a boy or man's name
Kim : a girl or woman's name

Page 22. **Knickerbocker glory** - an ice cream treat

Page 23. **go Kart** : a small motorized vehicle for fun or short distances

Page 24. **Kippers** : small fish

Page 25. **Knock** : strike a sounding blow, like on a door or window to call attention to - bump, strike, collide
Knot : intertwining rope, string, or a cord, to bunch up, or organized to hold or secure something
Koo : here - the name of the teacher
Kindergarten : a - class for young children between the ages of 4-6 year olds

Page 26. **Kite** - a large frame covered by material that is flown in the air by the wind at the end of a long string

Page 27. **Kennel** : a building or house to shelter animals like cats and dogs

Page 28. **Kimono** : loose, wide-sleeved robe that fastens at the waist with a sash - Japanese clothing
Koi : colorful fish of the carp family - goldfish?
Kelp : seaweed - that can be used for food

Page 29. **Knuckles** : the large joints in the middle of the hand - or to fall over?
Knobbly-knees : knees - the joint in the middle of the leg - knobbly - bumping bumps
Kokua : Hawaiian for 'Help'

Page 30. **Kanga Kendrick** : the male character here
Knapsack : canvas, nylon, leather bag for food or other items, supplies carried on one's back, usually for soldiers or hikers

Page 31. **Key** : small metal instrument that is cut to match or fit in a lock to lock and unlock the lock to secure items, to move a bolt and open

Paula Curtis-Taylorson Lives in Marston Mortaine England. She is a full-time secondary school teacher of English and English Literature. She was amongst the first of the initial students to graduate from the Uk's first BA (Hons) Creative Writing Program at the University of Bedfordshire.

Her first love is poetry and rhyme and she works hard to inspire and teach appreciation of the subject to all age groups. Many of her students have gone on to be successful writers.

A2Z Press LLC

A2Z Press LLC
published this work.
A2Z Press LLC is a
publishing company
created by Terrie Sizemore
for the purpose
of publishing literary works by new
and aspiring writers. All content is
G-rated. We welcome your submissions
of ideas for children's literature as well
as adult and self-help topics.
Science and medicine, holidays and
other interesting topics are all welcome.
Submit queries to sizemore3630@aol.com or
PO Box 582
Deleon Springs, FL 32130

Visit our Website

Visit terriesizemorestoryteller.com or bestlittleonlinebookstore.com for our latest titles and gifts for everyone.

www.ingramcontent.com/pod-product-compliance
Lightning Source LLC
Chambersburg PA
CBHW041523120626
46551CB00018B/2544